© 1989 Franklin Watts

First published in the USA by
Franklin Watts Inc
387 Park Avenue South
New York
NY 10016

US ISBN: 0-531-10728-0
Library of Congress Catalog
Card Number 89-5250


**Series Editor**
Norman Barrett

**Designed by**
K and Co

**Photographs by**
Action Plus
Daytona International Speedway
Berggren-Lopez Publications
Keith Clark/Action Plus
Renault Cars Ltd
Thrust Cars Ltd

**Technical Consultant**
Marcus Pye

# The Picture World of

# Racing Cars

C. J. Norman

## CONTENTS

## Franklin Watts

London • New York • Sydney • Toronto

# Introduction

Motor racing is an exciting sport. In most of its forms the drivers race cars around a circuit or track. Many different types of cars are raced.

In Formula One racing, high-powered, open-wheel cars roar around the track as they battle for the lead.

The smallest racing cars are karts. Boys and girls can take part in karting from about the age of eight.

△ The sparks fly as a Formula One racing car scorches around the bend. Formula One is the top class of motor racing. A formula is a set of rules that controls the power and size of racing cars.

▷ Stock car racing is for hard-top cars based on regular road automobiles. It takes place mainly on banked (sloping), oval tracks.

◁ People of all ages enjoy racing karts. These junior drivers are only eight or nine years old.

7

# Grand Prix cars

"Grand Prix" is French for "big prize." Formula One cars take part in Grand Prix races. These are important events and are held in countries all over the world. Manufacturers enter their cars in these events.

▽ A Ferrari, one of the most famous of all racing car makes. Racing cars use wide, smooth tires called "slicks."

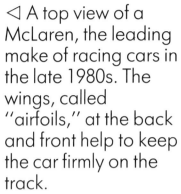
◁ A top view of a McLaren, the leading make of racing cars in the late 1980s. The wings, called "airfoils," at the back and front help to keep the car firmly on the track.

◁ A Williams car takes a sharp bend. The words and symbols seen all over racing cars are advertisements for products. The makers of these products sponsor the sport by providing money to help build the cars and for prizes.

# The drivers

Driving a racing car calls for great skill. Drivers need quick reflexes, especially when cornering at speed or when racing close to other cars.

Drivers wear safety belts, helmets and protective clothing. If a driver misjudges a bend at speed by a fraction of a second, his car might skid off the track, or he might crash into another car.

▽ Drivers wear very strong safety helmets with a visor that covers the eyes. They are strapped in with safety belts, and a metal roll bar behind their head protects them if the car turns over.

△ A driver adjusts his fireproof face mask. Drivers wear fireproof clothing to give them extra protection from sparks or in case they are caught in a fire.

Motor racing is a dangerous sport. Despite all the safety precautions, some drivers suffer serious injury or even death.

Racing drivers compete for the thrills and because they love motor racing. The top drivers are among the best paid competitors in any sport.

△ Brazilian driver Ayrton Senna, the 1988 World Champion, holds up the winner's trophy after coming in first in the British Grand Prix that year.

# The team

In motor racing, the drivers take the risks and earn the glory. But behind each driver is a manufacturer and a team of designers and mechanics.

It costs a fortune to build a racing car and run it in world championship races. The manufacturer depends on money from advertising as well as help from makers of parts such as tires.

△ The Williams racing team – car, driver and mechanics.

◁ A mechanic works on an engine in the workshop. Engines need careful attention after each race. They are regularly rebuilt. Designers and mechanics are always trying to make their cars run a little better.

▽ Mechanics make last-minute adjustments to a car before a race. This is done in an area called the pits, by the side of the track.

# The circuits

Grand Prix races are held on tracks throughout the world.

Most tracks are specially built circuits in the country, such as Silverstone, in England, and Monza, in Italy. The Adelaide and Monaco Grand Prix races are held on street circuits.

▽ The Hungarian Grand Prix is held on a newly built road track a few kilometres outside Budapest. The circuit has many sharp bends and is 4 km (2.5 miles) long.

▷ A car takes a hairpin bend in the Monaco Grand Prix. The race is run on the streets of Monaco, a tiny country on the southern coast of France.

▽ The Monaco circuit includes a tunnel.

# The racing

In a Grand Prix race, the cars go around the track many times. On some tracks they do as many as 80 laps (circuits).

On all circuits there is at least one long stretch called a straight. There are also many twists and turns. These are designed to test the drivers' skills and the performance of the cars.

△ Cars start a race in rows of two on a marked section of the track called the grid. Their place on the starting grid is determined by how fast they lap the track on qualifying runs.

▷ Drivers use all their skills to steer around corners as fast as possible without losing control of their cars.

▷ Racing tires are designed for speed and do not always last a whole race. In some Grand Prix, the cars need to stop in the pits for a change of tires. A good team can change a complete set of tires in under 15 seconds.

◁ Safety barriers, designed to prevent serious injury to drivers and the people watching, line the tracks in case of skids or crashes.

▷ Officials called track marshalls use colored flags to signal to the drivers.
A yellow flag means danger ahead.

▽ The black and white checkered flag signals the end of the race.

# Other motor sports

Motor racing takes different forms in many parts of the world. The competitions vary and so do the cars.

Some races last for thousands of miles, others for just a few seconds. The cars come in all shapes and sizes.

△ Powerful sports cars take part in a 1,000 km (620 mile) race. There is a world championship for sports car drivers, with races in many countries. They are all long-distance events, and some include driving at night.

▷ "Banger" racing is for "souped up" old cars. Contact is allowed as the cars circle a small track. There are strict safety precautions, but many cars finish up as wrecks.

◁ Rally driving is not a true race. A rally often lasts several days and is divided into special stages. The drivers start at intervals. They must complete each stage in a set time, or they lose points. The driver has a navigator to read the route.

△ Stock car racing at Daytona, Florida. This popular form of racing takes place mainly on banked oval tracks. The cars are based on the latest models.

▷ Rallycross takes place on special circuits with changing surfaces. Drivers have to keep control of their cars as they move from tarmac to grass and even chalk and mud.

◁ Dirt Modified cars race on short, dirt tracks.

▽ Sprint car racing is another class specially designed for short circuits.

△ Drag racing takes place on a ¼-mile (402 meter) or ⅛-mile (201 meter) strip. It is a straight contest between two cars called dragsters.

◁ Two "funny cars" line up for a drag race. In this class, the cars have fiberglass bodies, which are copies of sedans. The fastest cars run on alcohol fuel.

Karting is like Grand Prix racing in miniature. The simplest kart has a small engine and no gear-box. The driver sits very close to the ground.

Racing takes place on all kinds of tracks, from about 200 meters (⅛ mile) to full motor racing circuits. There are world championships for some classes of karts.

▽ One of the more powerful karts taking part in a championship race. The fastest karts can reach speeds of 240 kp/h (150 mph).

# Facts

## Points

In Grand Prix races that count toward the World Drivers Championship, points are awarded to the first six finishers. The winner gets 9 points. The driver finishing second gets 6 points. Third place is worth 4 points, fourth 3, fifth 2 and sixth 1. The driver with most points at the end of the season from his best 11 results is the World Champion.

△ Tires with treads are used on wet tracks.

## Choice of tires

In dry weather, racing cars run on smooth tires called slicks. The whole surface of these tires is in contact with the track. They provide more grip and enable the car to corner faster. But they cannot be used on a wet track, because they push the water in front of them and then float on it.

On wet circuits, tires with a tread are used. The tread is a pattern cut into the tires, as used on regular road vehicles. Wet-weather tires do not grip the track as well as slicks, but the grooves allow any surface water to escape.

△ A racing slick – a wide, smooth tire used on dry circuits.

26

## Champion

In 1985, Alain Prost became the first Frenchman to win the World Drivers Championship. With more than 35 Grands Prix victories to his name, he has won more than any other driver.

△ Alain Prost, champion driver.

## Race against the clock

Special cars are built to break speed records. They do not race against each other, but are timed over a set course. To set the world land speed record, a car must make two runs in opposite directions over either a mile or a kilometer. The average of the two runs is taken.

Record-breaking cars now use jet or rocket engines. In a record attempt, the car has a flying start. That is, it gets up to full speed before passing the starting mark.

Cars built to break speed records are so fast that there are few places in the world that can provide the large expanse of hard, level ground needed.

△ British driver Richard Noble in his record-breaking car *Thrust 2*. He set a world land speed record of 1,019 kp/h (633 mph) in 1983. The record run took place on the flat, dry Black Rock Desert, in Nevada. This is one of the few places on earth suitable for record attempts.

27

# Glossary

**Airfoil**
A special part at the front or back of a racing car that helps to keep it firmly on the ground. Airfoils are designed so that the air rushing over the car pushes it downward.

**Banking**
Some tracks are sloped up toward the outside at bends. This is called banking. It helps cars to take the bends faster.

**Flying start**
Going past the starting point in motion.

**Formula One**
The top class of Grand Prix motor racing. A formula is a set of rules controlling the power and size of cars. There are several other formulas, or classes.

**Grand Prix**
An important international motor race. "Grand Prix" is French for "big prize."

**Grid**
A section of the track before the starting line. Places are marked on the grid for all the starters.

**Pits**
An area just off the track in which cars may be worked on or have their tires changed during a race.

**Slicks**
Wide, smooth tires used on racing cars to give good contact with the track. They have no tread. Slicks are not used on wet or dirt circuits.

**Straight**
Any long, straight part of a circuit where the cars can reach their maximum speed. Races usually start and finish on a straight.

**Tread**
The pattern cut into tires for use on loose or wet surfaces and dirt tracks or for normal road use.

# Index